DROP IT IN THE TO DO BASKET

1999 DESK CALENDAR

DILBERT™

BY SCOTT ADAMS

Andrews McMeel
Publishing

an Andrews McMeel Universal company
Kansas City

 For information write Andrews McMeel Publishing, an Andrews McMeel Universal company, 4520 Main Street, Kansas City, Missouri 64111.

www.andrewsmcmeel.com

ISBN: 0-8362-5523-2

E-Mail: SCOTTADAMS@AOL.COM
www.dilbert.com

Are you interested in receiving the official publication of
DOGBERT'S NEW RULING CLASS (the DNRC)?

It's FREE! Subscribe automatically via e-mail:

Address: LISTSERV@listserv.unitedmedia.com
Subject: Newsletter
Message: SUBSCRIBE Dilbert_News YourFirstName YourLastName
(Fill in your first and last name only)

Or send your name and address to:
THE DILBERT NEWSLETTER
c/o United Media
200 Madison Avenue
New York, NY 10016

1999

JANUARY

S	M	T	W	T	F	S
					1	2
3	4	5	6	7	8	9
10	11	12	13	14	15	16
17	18	19	20	21	22	23
24	25	26	27	28	29	30
31						

FEBRUARY

S	M	T	W	T	F	S
	1	2	3	4	5	6
7	8	9	10	11	12	13
14	15	16	17	18	19	20
21	22	23	24	25	26	27
28						

MARCH

S	M	T	W	T	F	S
	1	2	3	4	5	6
7	8	9	10	11	12	13
14	15	16	17	18	19	20
21	22	23	24	25	26	27
28	29	30	31			

APRIL

S	M	T	W	T	F	S
				1	2	3
4	5	6	7	8	9	10
11	12	13	14	15	16	17
18	19	20	21	22	23	24
25	26	27	28	29	30	

MAY

S	M	T	W	T	F	S
						1
2	3	4	5	6	7	8
9	10	11	12	13	14	15
16	17	18	19	20	21	22
23	24	25	26	27	28	29
30	31					

JUNE

S	M	T	W	T	F	S
		1	2	3	4	5
6	7	8	9	10	11	12
13	14	15	16	17	18	19
20	21	22	23	24	25	26
27	28	29	30			

JULY

S	M	T	W	T	F	S
				1	2	3
4	5	6	7	8	9	10
11	12	13	14	15	16	17
18	19	20	21	22	23	24
25	26	27	28	29	30	31

AUGUST

S	M	T	W	T	F	S
1	2	3	4	5	6	7
8	9	10	11	12	13	14
15	16	17	18	19	20	21
22	23	24	25	26	27	28
29	30	31				

SEPTEMBER

S	M	T	W	T	F	S
			1	2	3	4
5	6	7	8	9	10	11
12	13	14	15	16	17	18
19	20	21	22	23	24	25
26	27	28	29	30		

OCTOBER

S	M	T	W	T	F	S
					1	2
3	4	5	6	7	8	9
10	11	12	13	14	15	16
17	18	19	20	21	22	23
24	25	26	27	28	29	30
31						

NOVEMBER

S	M	T	W	T	F	S
	1	2	3	4	5	6
7	8	9	10	11	12	13
14	15	16	17	18	19	20
21	22	23	24	25	26	27
28	29	30				

DECEMBER

S	M	T	W	T	F	S
			1	2	3	4
5	6	7	8	9	10	11
12	13	14	15	16	17	18
19	20	21	22	23	24	25
26	27	28	29	30	31	

DILBERT®
BY
SCOTT ADAMS
WALLY, YOU NEVER REALLY ANSWERED THE QUESTION I LEFT ON YOUR VOICE-MAIL.
IS THIS A CASE OF SIMPLE INCOMPETENCE OR A PREVIEW OF SOMETHING FAR MORE SINISTER?
S. Adams
IT'S THE SINISTER ONE
I'VE ADOPTED A DEFENSIVE STRATEGY. I'M WITHHOLDING INFORMATION TO MAKE MYSELF APPEAR MORE VALUABLE.
NOW I ONLY RETURN PHONE CALLS LATE AT NIGHT AND LEAVE INCOMPLETE ANSWERS.
IN PERSON, I ACT OVERWORKED AND IRRATIONAL SO PEOPLE STOP ASKING QUESTIONS.
1-1-95 © 1994 United Feature Syndicate, Inc.
IF CORNERED, I SIGH DEEPLY AND RECOUNT OLD WAR STORIES THAT DON'T RELATE TO THE QUESTION.
GOT IT!
NO CO-WORKER CAN THWART ME!
WHAT IF THEY TEAM UP?

NOTES

DEC-JAN

28 MONDAY

29 TUESDAY

30 WEDNESDAY

31 THURSDAY

FRIDAY 1
NEW YEAR'S DAY

SATURDAY 2

SUNDAY 3

DECEMBER 1998

S	M	T	W	T	F	S
		1	2	3	4	5
6	7	8	9	10	11	12
13	14	15	16	17	18	19
20	21	22	23	24	25	26
27	28	29	30	31		

JANUARY

S	M	T	W	T	F	S
					1	2
3	4	5	6	7	8	9
10	11	12	13	14	15	16
17	18	19	20	21	22	23
24	25	26	27	28	29	30
31						

DILBERT®
BY
SCOTT ADAMS
CONGRATULATIONS!
YOU'VE BEEN NAMED "FLOOR WARDEN."
S. Adams
IN THE EVENT OF A FIRE WE'LL RELY ON YOUR LEADERSHIP TO GET US OUT SAFELY.
LET ME SEE IF I UNDERSTAND THIS . . .
YOU'RE THE LEADER WHEN IT INVOLVES UNINFORMED DECISIONS IN RETURN FOR HUGE STOCK OPTIONS.
BUT I'M THE LEADER WHEN IT COMES TO RISKING DEATH IN A HIGHRISE INFERNO WHILE YOU SCRAMBLE OVER THE ASHEN BACKS OF FALLEN CO-WORKERS.
© 1995 United Feature Syndicate, Inc.
1-8
WHAT MAKES YOU THINK YOUR LIFE IS WORTH MORE THAN MINE?
I'VE GOT STOCK OPTIONS AND YOU'RE A FLOOR WARDEN.
DON'T EXPECT ANY CPR.

NOTES

JANUARY

4 MONDAY

5 TUESDAY

6 WEDNESDAY

7 THURSDAY

FRIDAY 8

SATURDAY 9

SUNDAY 10

JANUARY

S	M	T	W	T	F	S
					1	2
3	4	5	6	7	8	9
10	11	12	13	14	15	16
17	18	19	20	21	22	23
24	25	26	27	28	29	30
31						

DILBERT
BY
SCOTT ADAMS
OUR NEW PHILOSOPHY IS "WE DO IT RIGHT THE FIRST TIME."
S. Adams
THIS WILL INSPIRE YOU TO HIGHER QUALITY BECAUSE YOU'LL REALIZE MISTAKES ARE NOT TOLERATED.
QUESTION.
SINCE MISTAKES ARE INEVITABLE, WOULDN'T YOUR PHILOSOPHY INSPIRE US TO AVOID COMPLETING ANYTHING?
WE'LL BE PARALYZED BY THE FEAR OF MISTAKES, VICTIMS OF OUR OWN UNREALISTIC PHILOSOPHY.
YOU MIGHT AS WELL HAVE A PHILOSOPHY THAT SAYS "WE PUNISH ANYBODY WHO DOES ANYTHING."
© 1995 United Feature Syndicate, Inc.
1-15
I VALUE YOUR OPINION.
WALLY, I WANT YOU TO MAKE SOME POSTERS THAT SAY "WE DO IT RIGHT THE FIRST TIME."
WALLY'S PARALYZED.
NEXT ITEM: WHY IS EMPLOYEE MORALE SO LOW?

NOTES

JANUARY

11 MONDAY

12 TUESDAY

13 WEDNESDAY

14 THURSDAY

FRIDAY 15

SATURDAY 16

SUNDAY 17

JANUARY

S	M	T	W	T	F	S
					1	2
3	4	5	6	7	8	9
10	11	12	13	14	15	16
17	18	19	20	21	22	23
24	25	26	27	28	29	30
31						

DILBERT®
BY
SCOTT ADAMS
HOW NATURE PROTECTS WEAK PRODUCTS
S. Adams
FIRST, THE ENGINEER PADS HIS SCHEDULE
SIX MONTHS?
AT LEAST.
ONE MONTH TO BUILD THE PRODUCT AND FIVE MONTHS TO PLAY "DOOM" ON MY COMPUTER.
THEN THE MANAGER PADS THE SCHEDULE AS A CLEVER NEGOTIATING PLOY.
ONE YEAR... UNLESS YOU ADD PEOPLE TO MY TINY EMPIRE.
THEN THE VICE PRESIDENT PADS THE SCHEDULE TO AVOID LOOKING BAD TO THE PRESIDENT.
EIGHTEEN MONTHS.
MEANWHILE, THE SALES PEOPLE ARE MAKING UP NUMBERS BECAUSE NOBODY TELLS THEM ANYTHING.
TWO MONTHS... AND IT SOLVES EVERY PROBLEM YOU HAVE!
© 1995 United Feature Syndicate, Inc.
THIS CAUSES THE CUSTOMERS TO DEVELOP IRRATIONAL DESIRE FOR THE PRODUCT.
GIVE ME THE "BETA" TEST VERSION IN ONE MONTH.
THUS NATURE DISGUISES WEAK PRODUCTS AS "BETA".
CARDBOARD? THAT'S STUPID.
OH... THEN IT'S BETA.

NOTES

JANUARY

18 MONDAY

MARTIN LUTHER KING JR.'S
BIRTHDAY (OBSERVED)

19 TUESDAY

20 WEDNESDAY

21 THURSDAY

FRIDAY 22

SATURDAY 23

SUNDAY 24

JANUARY

S	M	T	W	T	F	S
					1	2
3	4	5	6	7	8	9
10	11	12	13	14	15	16
17	18	19	20	21	22	23
24	25	26	27	28	29	30
31						

DILBERT®
BY
SCOTT ADAMS
I'LL BE DOWN AT THE LAKE, PUSHING PEOPLE IN.
YOU NEED A NEW HOBBY, DOGBERT.
IT'S A SPORT!
HAVING ANY LUCK TODAY?
YEAH, I GOT ME A PRETTY ONE. YOU SHOULD HAVE SEEN IT FLOPPING AROUND. BEAUTIFUL!
BEAUTIFUL?? ARE YOU SAYING THERE'S BEAUTY IN CAUSING A LOWER FORM OF LIFE TO SUFFER?
ONLY IF IT'S A BIG ONE.
HOW MUCH DO YOU WEIGH?
OH, ABOUT 210 POUNDS, I RECKON.
WOULD YOU MIND FLOPPING AROUND SOME MORE?
IT'S BEAUTIFUL.
© 1995 United Feature Syndicate, Inc.

NOTES

JANUARY

25 MONDAY

26 TUESDAY

27 WEDNESDAY

28 THURSDAY

FRIDAY 29

SATURDAY 30

SUNDAY 31

JANUARY

S	M	T	W	T	F	S
					1	2
3	4	5	6	7	8	9
10	11	12	13	14	15	16
17	18	19	20	21	22	23
24	25	26	27	28	29	30
31						

DILBERT®
BY SCOTT ADAMS
DOGBERT EXPLAINS LEADERSHIP
LEADERS START THEIR CAREERS AS MORONS.
S. Adams
THEY ARE DRAWN TO MEETINGS LIKE MOTHS TO A PORCH LIGHT.
THE SUCCESSFUL MORON WILL HAVE A VERY HIGH BLADDER-TO-BRAIN RATIO.
BRAIN
BLADDER
THEY PREVAIL IN ALL DECISIONS BECAUSE THEY ARE IMPERVIOUS TO LOGIC OR COFFEE.
LET'S DO IT MY WAY!
OKAY!
THESE QUALITIES ARE PERCEIVED AS LEADERSHIP.
YOU'RE PROMOTED!
2-5
© 1995 United Feature Syndicate, Inc.
AFTER SEVERAL PROMOTIONS THEIR JOB TENDS TO MATCH THEIR TALENTS.
I AWARD YOU THIS AWARD.
CONCLUSION: LEADERSHIP IS NATURE'S WAY OF REMOVING MORONS FROM THE PRODUCTIVE FLOW.

NOTES

FEBRUARY

1 MONDAY

2 TUESDAY
GROUNDHOG DAY

3 WEDNESDAY

4 THURSDAY

FRIDAY 5

SATURDAY 6

SUNDAY 7

FEBRUARY

S	M	T	W	T	F	S
	1	2	3	4	5	6
7	8	9	10	11	12	13
14	15	16	17	18	19	20
21	22	23	24	25	26	27
28						

DILBERT®
BY
SCOTT ADAMS
I'M PUTTING YOU ON THE STRATEGIC PLANNING TEAM.
IT'S LIKE WORK BUT WITHOUT THE SATISFACTION OF ACCOMPLISHING ANYTHING.
YOU'RE NEW, SO LET ME EXPLAIN HOW THIS WORKS.
WE HAVE MEETINGS AND TALK ABOUT THE COMPANY'S STRATEGY IN VAGUE EMOTIONAL TERMS.
IN TIME, WE CONVINCE OURSELVES THAT WE'RE MORE THAN MEDIOCRE THINKERS WHO SIT AROUND COMPLAINING.
2-12
WE START BELIEVING OUR OPINIONS WILL STEER THE COMPANY. WE FEEL IMPORTANT. WE FEEL **ALIVE**!!
© 1995 United Feature Syndicate, Inc.
THEN WE SNAP OUT OF IT AND MAKE VIEWGRAPHS THAT SAY WE SHOULD KEEP DOING WHAT WE'RE DOING.
I LIKE MAKING VIEW-GRAPHS.
ACTUALLY, WE USE LAST YEAR'S VIEWGRAPH

NOTES

FEBRUARY

8 MONDAY

9 TUESDAY

10 WEDNESDAY

11 THURSDAY

FRIDAY 12

SATURDAY 13

SUNDAY 14

VALENTINE'S DAY

FEBRUARY

S	M	T	W	T	F	S
	1	2	3	4	5	6
7	8	9	10	11	12	13
14	15	16	17	18	19	20
21	22	23	24	25	26	27
28						

DILBERT®
BY
SCOTT ADAMS
BOSS TYPES
FIND YOUR BOSS ON THIS HANDY REFERENCE.
S. ADAMS
HOSTAGE TAKER: TRAPS YOU IN YOUR CUBICLE AND TALKS YOUR EARS OFF.
BLAH BLAH
OW!!
FRAUD: USES VIGOROUS HEAD-NODDING TO SIMULATE COMPREHENSION.
THEN WE'LL SUBNET OUR I.P. ADDRESSES.
OH YEAH OH YEAH
MOTIVATIONAL LIAR: HAS NO CLUE WHAT YOU DO BUT SAYS YOU'RE THE BEST.
NOBODY CAN DO WHAT YOU DO!!
EXCEPT A MUSHROOM.
OVER PROMOTED: TRIES TO MASK INCOMPETENCE WITH POOR COMMUNICATION.
LET'S QUALITIZE OUR PARADIGM SO WE DON'T OVER INUNDATE WITH DATUMS.
WEASEL: TAKES CREDIT FOR YOUR HARD WORK.
THIS BONUS IS FOR BRILLIANTLY FORCING YOUR STAFF TO WORK 80 HOUR WEEKS.
IT WASN'T EASY!
2-19
© 1995 United Feature Syndicate, Inc.
MOSES: PERPETUALLY WAITS FOR CLEAR SIGNALS FROM ABOVE.
DON'T DO ANYTHING IMPORTANT YET.
NEVER HAVE.
PERFECT BOSS: DIES OF NATURAL CAUSES ON A THURSDAY AFTERNOON.
SHOULD WE DO SOMETHING?
THREE DAY WEEKEND!

NOTES

FEBRUARY

15 MONDAY
PRESIDENTS' DAY

16 TUESDAY

17 WEDNESDAY
ASH WEDNESDAY

18 THURSDAY

FRIDAY 19

SATURDAY 20

SUNDAY 21

FEBRUARY

S	M	T	W	T	F	S
	1	2	3	4	5	6
7	8	9	10	11	12	13
14	15	16	17	18	19	20
21	22	23	24	25	26	27
28						

DILBERT®
BY SCOTT ADAMS
HERE'S SOME NICE CHOCOLATE CAKE FOR YOU AND DOGBERT.
THANKS, MOM.
THANKS, MOM.
S. Adams
TELL ME ALL ABOUT YOUR JOB AT THE RAILROAD.
IT'S NOT A RAILROAD. I'M AN ENGINEER AT A BIG CORPORATION.
DO YOU FIX THE TYPEWRITERS WHEN THEY BREAK?
NO... TODAY I DEBUGGED A TCP/IP DRIVER FOR AN APPLICATION THAT RUNS OVER ISDN WITH BONDING.
YOU MEAN, ALL YOU DO IS SLAP A BRI ANALYZER ON A CIRCUIT AND LOOK FOR BAD PACKETS?
2-26
© 1995 United Feature Syndicate, Inc.
WELL... YEAH.
BUT IT'S REALLY HARD.
I WAS DOING OKAY UNTIL SHE OFFERED TO PAY MY TUITION TO TYPEWRITER REPAIR SCHOOL.
YOU SHOULDN'T HAVE COMPARED HER CAKE TO PACKING FOAM.

NOTES

FEBRUARY

22 MONDAY

23 TUESDAY

24 WEDNESDAY

25 THURSDAY

FRIDAY 26

SATURDAY 27

SUNDAY 28

FEBRUARY

S	M	T	W	T	F	S
	1	2	3	4	5	6
7	8	9	10	11	12	13
14	15	16	17	18	19	20
21	22	23	24	25	26	27
28						

DILBERT
BY
SCOTT ADAMS
WE'RE GOING DOWNTOWN TO PLAY "SECURITY GUARDS IN SPACE."
I DON'T WANT TO KNOW.
GEEK WEEK
S. Adams
LET'S TRY THAT BUILD-ING.
LUNCH
I'LL NEED TO SEE YOUR I.D. BADGE, SIR.
LOOK FAST!! THERE IT IS!! NOT A PACK OF MATCHES!!
OKAY
ZIP!
I'LL HAVE TO SEARCH YOUR LUNCH BOX.
IT'S JUST A BUNCH OF WIRES AND GIZMOS.
YOU'RE MAKING ME SO HUNGRY
LUNCH
© 1995 United Feature Syndicate, Inc.
COULD YOU WATCH MY LUNCH WHILE I TAKE THE CART BACK TO MY CAR?
3-5
I FEEL BAD, BUT IT'S THE ONLY WAY TO TEST IF SPACE TRAVEL IS SAFE FOR US ANIMALS.
I FEEL SAFER ALREADY.

NOTES

MARCH

1 MONDAY

2 TUESDAY
PURIM

3 WEDNESDAY

4 THURSDAY

FRIDAY 5

SATURDAY 6

SUNDAY 7

MARCH

S	M	T	W	T	F	S
	1	2	3	4	5	6
7	8	9	10	11	12	13
14	15	16	17	18	19	20
21	22	23	24	25	26	27
28	29	30	31			

DILBERT®
BY
SCOTT ADAMS
DID YOU REVIEW MY DRAFT DOCUMENTATION YET?
UH... I'LL GET TO IT SOON.
S. Adams
THAT'S WHAT YOU'VE BEEN SAYING SINCE JULY!!
I KNOW I'M ONLY A LOWLY TECHNICAL WRITER AND YOU'RE A BIG IMPORTANT ENGINEER...
BUT IS IT TOO MUCH TO ASK FOR YOU TO GLANCE AT THE FRUITS OF MY LABORS?!!!
FIVE LOUSY MINUTES IS ALL IT WOULD TAKE TO VALIDATE MY VALUE ON THIS PLANET! READ IT, YOU FETID PILE OF COMPOST!!
OKAY, OKAY! I'LL READ IT RIGHT NOW!
3-12
© 1995 United Feature Syndicate, Inc.
THESE PAGES ARE BLANK! YOU'VE BEEN BLUFFING FOR MONTHS!
I THINK I'LL GO HAVE A YUMMY COMPOST SALAD WITH DELICIOUS FETID CHEESE
I'M GOING TO LOOK UP THOSE WORDS.

NOTES

MARCH

8 MONDAY

9 TUESDAY

10 WEDNESDAY

11 THURSDAY

FRIDAY 12

SATURDAY 13

SUNDAY 14

MARCH

S	M	T	W	T	F	S
	1	2	3	4	5	6
7	8	9	10	11	12	13
14	15	16	17	18	19	20
21	22	23	24	25	26	27
28	29	30	31			

DILBERT®
BY
SCOTT ADAMS
SO... OKAY, GREAT...
ALRIGHT THEN...
S. Adams
I'M TRAPPED IN THE MEETING THAT WOULD NOT CONCLUDE!!
I'M TOO POLITE TO SAY "WE'RE DONE. PLEASE LEAVE."
LIKE I SAID BEFORE...
OH NO! I MISSED THE WINDOW – HE'S REITERATING!!!
SO...OKAY, GREAT...
ALRIGHT THEN...
MAYBE IF I SHAKE HIS HAND HE'LL LEAVE.
BUT LIKE I SAID BEFORE...
3-19
© 1995 United Feature Syndicate, Inc.
NOOOOOOOO!!
...THEN THERE WAS SORT OF A LONG AWKWARD PAUSE...
SO... OKAY, GREAT...

NOTES

MARCH

15 MONDAY

16 TUESDAY

17 WEDNESDAY

ST. PATRICK'S DAY

18 THURSDAY

FRIDAY 19

SATURDAY 20

SUNDAY 21

MARCH

S	M	T	W	T	F	S
	1	2	3	4	5	6
7	8	9	10	11	12	13
14	15	16	17	18	19	20
21	22	23	24	25	26	27
28	29	30	31			

DILBERT®
BY SCOTT ADAMS
PLEASE ENTER PHOTOCOPIER ACCESS CODE.
S. Adams
WHAT'S THE CODE FOR THIS MACHINE?
THAT'S PROPRIETARY INFORMATION.
WE WORK FOR THE SAME COMPANY. MY CUBICLE IS DOWN THE HALL.
I HAVE NO WAY OF VERIFYING YOUR CLAIM. ANYBODY COULD COME IN HERE AND SAY THAT.
ASK ME A QUESTION THAT ONLY AN EMPLOYEE OF THIS COMPANY COULD ANSWER.
OKAY.
WHAT IS THE ACCESS CODE FOR THIS COPIER?
3-26
© 1995 United Feature Syndicate, Inc.
SOB
I JUST HAVE ONE...

NOTES

MARCH

22 MONDAY

23 TUESDAY

24 WEDNESDAY

25 THURSDAY

FRIDAY 26

SATURDAY 27

SUNDAY 28
PALM SUNDAY

MARCH

S	M	T	W	T	F	S
	1	2	3	4	5	6
7	8	9	10	11	12	13
14	15	16	17	18	19	20
21	22	23	24	25	26	27
28	29	30	31			

DILBERT®
BY
SCOTT ADAMS
I'D LIKE YOU GUYS TO CHECK ANNE'S ADVERTISING MATERIALS FOR TECHNICAL ACCURACY.
S. Adams
IS THIS SUPPOSED TO BE FUNNY?
I DON'T GET IT.
I'M ONLY LOOKING FOR TECHNICAL HELP HERE.
HEY! MAYBE YOU COULD SAY SOMETHING ABOUT THOSE WARNING TAGS ON MATTRESSES! NOW THAT WOULD BE FUNNY!
OR HOW ABOUT THE FACT THAT YOU CAN'T LOOK UP SOMETHING IN THE DICTIONARY IF YOU CAN'T SPELL IT? THAT'S FUNNY!
YOU'RE ENGINEERS, NOT COMEDIANS!! I WANT TECHNICAL HELP!!!
4-2
© 1995 United Feature Syndicate, Inc.
THIS GUY HAS AN XP-6. IT SHOULD BE AN XP-7.
THAT'S BETTER.
AND HE SHOULD BE SAYING "I'VE FALLEN AND I CAN'T GET UP."
WHO PICKED THESE COLORS?

NOTES

MARCH/APRIL

29 MONDAY

30 TUESDAY

31 WEDNESDAY

1 THURSDAY
PASSOVER

FRIDAY 2
GOOD FRIDAY

SATURDAY 3

SUNDAY 4
EASTER

MARCH

S	M	T	W	T	F	S
	1	2	3	4	5	6
7	8	9	10	11	12	13
14	15	16	17	18	19	20
21	22	23	24	25	26	27
28	29	30	31			

APRIL

S	M	T	W	T	F	S
				1	2	3
4	5	6	7	8	9	10
11	12	13	14	15	16	17
18	19	20	21	22	23	24
25	26	27	28	29	30	

DILBERT®
BY
SCOTT ADAMS
WE RANKED ALL THE ENGINEERS FROM BEST TO WORST.
S. Adams
WE PLAN TO GET RID OF THE BOTTOM 10%. THAT INCLUDES YOU, WALLY.
YOUR PLAN IS LOGICALLY FLAWED.
IF YOU FIRE THE BOTTOM 10%, YOU'LL STILL HAVE A BOTTOM 10%.
YOU'LL FIRE AND FIRE BUT THERE WILL ALWAYS BE A BOTTOM 10%, UNTIL FINALLY...
WHEN LESS THAN TEN PEOPLE ARE LEFT YOU'LL HAVE TO FIRE BODY PARTS INSTEAD OF WHOLE PEOPLE!!!
© 1995 United Feature Syndicate, Inc.
WE'LL HAVE TORSOS AND GLANDS WANDERING AROUND UNABLE TO USE KEYBOARDS... BLOOD AND BILE EVERYWHERE!!!
4-9
HOW'D IT GO?
HE FIRED MY HAIR.

NOTES

APRIL

5 MONDAY
EASTER MONDAY (CANADA)

6 TUESDAY

7 WEDNESDAY

8 THURSDAY

FRIDAY 9

SATURDAY 10

SUNDAY 11

APRIL

S	M	T	W	T	F	S
				1	2	3
4	5	6	7	8	9	10
11	12	13	14	15	16	17
18	19	20	21	22	23	24
25	26	27	28	29	30	

DILBERT®
BY
SCOTT ADAMS
LOOKS LIKE SOMEBODY HAS A JOB INTERVIEW.
SHHH
S. Adams
YOUR RÉSUMÉ IS IMPRESSIVE. I ONLY HAVE ONE QUESTION.
WHAT DO YOU CONSIDER YOUR BIGGEST FAULT?
SOMETIMES I WORK TOO HARD.
GOOD ONE
WHY IS THAT A FAULT?
WELL... UH... I WORK SO HARD THAT I FORGET TO EAT AND BATHE FOR DAYS. EVENTUALLY I STARVE TO DEATH AT MY DESK.
4-16
© 1995 United Feature Syndicate, Inc.
I BECOME A BLOATED, STINKING CORPSE. INSECTS BREED IN MY BODY. I SPREAD DISEASE TO THE ENTIRE COMPANY.
HOW DID IT GO?
THEY WANT SOMEBODY HUNGRIER.

NOTES

APRIL

12 MONDAY

13 TUESDAY

14 WEDNESDAY

15 THURSDAY

FRIDAY 16

SATURDAY 17

SUNDAY 18

APRIL

S	M	T	W	T	F	S
				1	2	3
4	5	6	7	8	9	10
11	12	13	14	15	16	17
18	19	20	21	22	23	24
25	26	27	28	29	30	

DILBERT®
BY
SCOTT ADAMS
YOU'LL BE PERFORMING A "TURING TEST" ON OUR NEW ARTIFICIAL INTELLIGENCE SOFTWARE.
TRY TO DETERMINE IF THE RESPONSES ON YOUR SCREEN COME FROM OUR COMPUTER OR A HUMAN IN THE NEXT ROOM.
S. Adams
I'LL ASK IT TO WRITE A STRATEGY FOR OUR COMPANY.
"OUR STRATEGY IS TO VISIONIZE QUALITY RESOURCES THAT ENHANCE EARNINGS."
HMM
I'LL ASK IT HOW TO MOTIVATE EMPLOYEES.
"REORGANIZE OFTEN TO IMPROVE FOCUS. REDEFINE WORK AS 'OPPORTUNITY' AND INCREASE IT DAILY. TAKE TIME TO ASK FOR OPINIONS THEN EXPLAIN WHY THEY'RE WRONG."
4-23
© 1995 United Feature Syndicate, Inc.
IT MUST BE A COMPUTER BECAUSE THERE'S NO HUMAN INTELLIGENCE.
UNLESS...
NICE TRY, BOSS.

NOTES

APRIL

19 MONDAY

20 TUESDAY

21 WEDNESDAY
SECRETARIES DAY

22 THURSDAY

FRIDAY 23

SATURDAY 24

SUNDAY 25

APRIL

S	M	T	W	T	F	S
				1	2	3
4	5	6	7	8	9	10
11	12	13	14	15	16	17
18	19	20	21	22	23	24
25	26	27	28	29	30	

DILBERT®
BY
SCOTT ADAMS
LET ME INTRODUCE YOU TO ONE OF OUR ENGINEERS.
S. Adams
KAREN IS OUR NEW VICE PRESIDENT. AND YOU ARE...?
DILBERT: VALUED EMPLOYEE.
I BELIEVE IN OPEN COMMUNICATIONS, DILBERT. FEEL FREE TO TALK ABOUT ANY-THING.
UH-OH
SO, WHAT WERE YOU WORKING ON?
OH-NO
WELL... I WAS JUST SENDING AN E-MAIL TO SOMEBODY WHO SITS BY A WINDOW TO ASK IF IT'S RAIN-ING.
IF IT'S RAINING I'LL FASHION A RAINCOAT FROM A LARGE TRASH BAG.
WATCH.
© 1995 United Feature Syndicate, Inc.
4-30
THREE HOLES AND YOU'RE READY TO GO!
ARE YOU PLANNING TO GO OUT AT LUNCH?
ONLY IF IT RAINS.

NOTES

APRIL/MAY

26 MONDAY

27 TUESDAY

28 WEDNESDAY

29 THURSDAY

FRIDAY 30

SATURDAY 1

SUNDAY 2

APRIL

S	M	T	W	T	F	S
				1	2	3
4	5	6	7	8	9	10
11	12	13	14	15	16	17
18	19	20	21	22	23	24
25	26	27	28	29	30	

MAY

S	M	T	W	T	F	S
						1
2	3	4	5	6	7	8
9	10	11	12	13	14	15
16	17	18	19	20	21	22
23	24	25	26	27	28	29
30	31					

DILBERT®
BY
SCOTT ADAMS
THE 7 HABITS OF
HIGHLY
DEFECTIVE
PEOPLE
OW!
S. Adams
1. IGNORE ANY SIGNS OF DISCOMFORT IN OTHERS.
BUT HEY, I'VE BEEN DOING ALL OF THE TALKING.
2. USE HUMOR TO BELITTLE PEOPLE IN PUBLIC.
OUR NEWEST TEAM MEMBER HAS MOVIE STAR LOOKS. SPECIFICALLY, LASSIE.
3. TREAT ALL COMPLAINTS AS THE COMPLAINER'S FAULT.
YOU DON'T MOTIVATE ME.
MAYBE YOU SHOULD SEE A THERAPIST.
4. SHOW UP LATE AND RAISE CONTROVERSIAL ISSUES.
I THINK WE SHOULD LICENSE "BARNEY" AS OUR MASCOT.
5. GIVE ADVICE ON THINGS YOU DON'T UNDERSTAND.
TRY WRITING SOME ASSEMBLY LINE CODE HERE.
© 1995 United Feature Syndicate, Inc.
5-7
6. USE COMPLIMENTS TO SHOW YOUR PREJUDICES.
OOH, NICE CRISP PHOTO-COPY, ALICE. I DON'T THINK A MAN COULD HAVE DONE IT BETTER!
7. THINK THE COMICS ARE NOT ABOUT YOU
HEE HEE! LOOK AT THE HAIR ON THAT GUY!

NOTES

MAY

3 MONDAY

4 TUESDAY

5 WEDNESDAY

6 THURSDAY

FRIDAY 7

SATURDAY 8

SUNDAY 9
MOTHER'S DAY

MAY

S	M	T	W	T	F	S
						1
2	3	4	5	6	7	8
9	10	11	12	13	14	15
16	17	18	19	20	21	22
23	24	25	26	27	28	29
30	31					

DILBERT®
BY
SCOTT ADAMS
WRITE UP YOUR ACCOMPLISHMENTS SO I CAN DECIDE WHO GETS RAISES THIS YEAR.
S. Adams
ARE YOU SAYING OUR RAISES WILL DEPEND ON OUR ABILITY TO LIE ABOUT OUR ACHIEVEMENTS?
NO, THERE'S ALSO FAVORITISM.
AND DON'T FORGET THE IMPORTANCE OF MINIMIZING THE ACCOMPLISHMENTS OF OTHERS.
"THIS YEAR I SAVED A BILLION DOLLARS IN WAYS WHICH ARE IMPOSSIBLE TO VERIFY."
"WHILE THE OTHERS PLOTTED AGAINST YOU, I WAS APPLYING AN INVISIBLE RUST INHIBITOR TO YOUR CAR."
© 1995 United Feature Syndicate, Inc.
5-14
I CAN DROP THOSE OFF FOR YOU.
THANKS.
HAVE YOU NOTICED SHE'S THE ONLY ONE WHO EVER GETS A RAISE?
IT'S AS IF SHE HAS THE ACCOMPLISHMENTS OF THREE PEOPLE.

NOTES

MAY

10 MONDAY

11 TUESDAY

12 WEDNESDAY

13 THURSDAY

FRIDAY 14

SATURDAY 15
ARMED FORCES DAY

SUNDAY 16

MAY

S	M	T	W	T	F	S
						1
2	3	4	5	6	7	8
9	10	11	12	13	14	15
16	17	18	19	20	21	22
23	24	25	26	27	28	29
30	31					

DILBERT®
BY
SCOTT ADAMS
HERE'S THE COMPANY VISION AND BUSINESS PLAN.
S. Adams
"VISION: EMPOWERED EMPLOYEES WORKING TOWARD A COMMON PLAN."
SOUNDS GOOD.
BUT THE BUSINESS PLAN IS BLANK.
IT'S CONFI-DENTIAL.
HOW AM I SUPPOSED TO KNOW WHAT TO DO?
I'LL YELL AT YOU IF YOU DO THE WRONG THING.
I THOUGHT I WAS EMPOWERED.
DON'T BE SO LITERAL.
I'LL JUST KEEP DOING WHAT I WAS DOING.
NO!!! YOU FOOL!!!
© 1995 United Feature Syndicate, Inc.
5-21
WE'RE DOOMED, AREN'T WE?
I DON'T KNOW. I HAVEN'T SEEN THE PLAN.

NOTES

MAY

17 MONDAY

18 TUESDAY

19 WEDNESDAY

20 THURSDAY

FRIDAY 21

SATURDAY 22

SUNDAY 23

MAY

S	M	T	W	T	F	S
						1
2	3	4	5	6	7	8
9	10	11	12	13	14	15
16	17	18	19	20	21	22
23	24	25	26	27	28	29
30	31					

DILBERT®
BY
SCOTT ADAMS
I'M PUTTING YOU IN CHARGE OF PROJECT "BIFF."
DILBERT
"BIFF" STANDS FOR "BIG IMPROVEMENTS FOR FREE."
S. Adams
YOUR JOB IS TO RECOMMEND WAYS TO INCREASE PROFITS WITHOUT SPENDING MONEY OR CHANGING ANYTHING.
YOU HAVE TO SPEND MONEY TO MAKE MONEY.
IF WE HAD MONEY TO SPEND WE WOULDN'T NEED TO MAKE MONEY.
DUH
THE POINT IS THAT YOU CAN MAKE MORE MONEY THAN YOU SPEND.
I'M NOT FOLLOWING YOUR SO-CALLED "POINT."
5-28 © 1995 United Feature Syndicate, Inc.
LOGICALLY, ANYTHING I DON'T UNDERSTAND IS UNIMPORTANT.
HAVE YOUR REPORT TOMORROW.
SO, YOU RECOMMEND... REPLACING ALL MANAGERS WITH LAVA LAMPS.
HERE'S A FEW BUCKS FOR THE LAVA LAMPS.

NOTES

MAY

24 MONDAY
VICTORIA DAY (CANADA)

25 TUESDAY

26 WEDNESDAY

27 THURSDAY

FRIDAY 28

SATURDAY 29

SUNDAY 30

MAY

S	M	T	W	T	F	S
						1
2	3	4	5	6	7	8
9	10	11	12	13	14	15
16	17	18	19	20	21	22
23	24	25	26	27	28	29
30	31					

DILBERT®
BY
SCOTT ADAMS
YOUR COMPANY MAKES AN ATTRACTIVE LITTLE PRODUCT, JIM.
BUT WE'VE DECIDED TO GO WITH A VENDOR WHOSE PRODUCT ACTUALLY WORKS.
FOOLS!!! I'LL CRUSH YOU!!!
I'LL TELL YOUR BOSS YOU MADE A STUPID DECISION!! YOUR CAREERS WILL BE RUINED AND I'LL GET THE CONTRACT ANY-WAY!!
YOU CAN'T SCARE US! DO YOU THINK OUR BOSS WILL BELIEVE A VENDOR OVER HIS OWN LOYAL EMPLOYEES?
MUST... KEEP... A... STRAIGHT... FACE...
6-4
© 1995 United Feature Syndicate, Inc.
HA HA HA HA HA HA HA HA
WE'LL TAKE A MILLION UNITS.
TAKE TWO MILLION AND I'LL SEE THAT YOU GET NICE RAISES.

NOTES

MAY/JUNE

31 MONDAY

MEMORIAL DAY

1 TUESDAY

2 WEDNESDAY

3 THURSDAY

FRIDAY 4

SATURDAY 5

SUNDAY 6

MAY

S	M	T	W	T	F	S
						1
2	3	4	5	6	7	8
9	10	11	12	13	14	15
16	17	18	19	20	21	22
23	24	25	26	27	28	29
30	31					

JUNE

S	M	T	W	T	F	S
		1	2	3	4	5
6	7	8	9	10	11	12
13	14	15	16	17	18	19
20	21	22	23	24	25	26
27	28	29	30			

DILBERT®
BY
SCOTT ADAMS
LET'S GO AROUND THE CIRCLE AND SHARE WHAT WE LEARNED IN THE THREE-DAY WORKSHOP.
TEAM
S. Adams
AT FIRST I THOUGHT IT WAS A WASTE OF OUR TRAINING BUDGET...
THEN YOU ASKED US TO FORM TEAMS AND MAKE PAPER AIRPLANES WHILE BLINDFOLDED...
I DON'T KNOW IF IT WAS BECAUSE OF THE DARKNESS OR THE WAY WE SHARED OUR THOUGHTS ABOUT FLIGHT...
BUT SUDDENLY I FOUND UNCONDITIONAL LOVE FOR MY CO-WORKERS.
BE THEY ACCOUNTANTS, BE THEY MARKETEERS OR BE THEY SECRETARIES.
AS A RESULT, I'VE BECOME A COMPETITIVE LION, EAGER TO POUNCE ON MY WORKLOAD AND INCREASE STOCKHOLDER VALUES!!
© 1995 United Feature Syndicate, Inc.
6-11
THANK YOU, WALLY.
DILBERT, WHAT DID YOU LEARN?
I LEARNED THAT YOU SHOULDN'T PUT A LITTLE ERASER-PILOT IN YOUR PAPER AIRPLANE.
SOMEBODY NEEDS A GROUP HUG!

NOTES

JUNE

7 MONDAY

8 TUESDAY

9 WEDNESDAY

10 THURSDAY

FRIDAY 11

SATURDAY 12

SUNDAY 13

JUNE

S	M	T	W	T	F	S
		1	2	3	4	5
6	7	8	9	10	11	12
13	14	15	16	17	18	19
20	21	22	23	24	25	26
27	28	29	30			

DILBERT®
BY
SCOTT ADAMS
I'VE BEEN INVITED TO BE A GUEST ON "CROSSFIRE" ON CNN.
S. Adams
I'M THE ONLY CREATURE ON EARTH WHO HASN'T ALREADY BEEN ON TELEVISION.
CAN YOU TEACH ME HOW TO DEBATE ON TELEVISION, DOGBERT?
OKAY
FIRST, RATBERT, ASSUME EVERYBODY HAS THE SAME DESIRES AND EXPERIENCES AS YOU.
ABSORB ABSORB
THEREFORE, IF THEY DISAGREE WITH YOU THEY MUST BE STUPID.
I THINK YOU'RE OVER-SIMPLIFYING, DOGBERT.
© 1995 United Feature Syndicate, Inc.
6-18
WHAT WAS THAT OPINION, RATBERT?
STUPID!
YOU'RE READY FOR "CROSSFIRE," RATBERT.
I USUALLY LIKE THE SAME MOVIES AS THE FAT ONE.

NOTES

JUNE

14 MONDAY
FLAG DAY

15 TUESDAY

16 WEDNESDAY

17 THURSDAY

FRIDAY 18

SATURDAY 19

SUNDAY 20
FATHER'S DAY

JUNE

S	M	T	W	T	F	S
		1	2	3	4	5
6	7	8	9	10	11	12
13	14	15	16	17	18	19
20	21	22	23	24	25	26
27	28	29	30			

DILBERT
BY
SCOTT ADAMS
TAKE CARE OF THIS, ALICE.
S. Adams
"TAKE CARE OF THIS"? THIS WOULD DOUBLE MY WORKLOAD.
I'VE ALREADY GOT SO MANY PROJECTS THAT I CAN'T DO ANYTHING USEFUL WITH ANY OF THEM.
BUT IF SUCCESS IS IMPOSSIBLE THEN...
I'M...FREE.
FREE! FREE! HA HA HA HA HA
THE RESULT WILL BE THE SAME NO MATTER WHAT I DO! YES YES YES
© 1995 United Feature Syndicate, Inc.
6-25
HONK HONK!
MOVING ALONG...WE NEED TO INVENTORY OUR OFFICE EQUIP-MENT.
SOUNDS LIKE A JOB FOR ALICE.

NOTES

JUNE

21 MONDAY

FRIDAY 25

22 TUESDAY

SATURDAY 26

23 WEDNESDAY

SUNDAY 27

24 THURSDAY

JUNE

S	M	T	W	T	F	S
		1	2	3	4	5
6	7	8	9	10	11	12
13	14	15	16	17	18	19
20	21	22	23	24	25	26
27	28	29	30			

DILBERT®
BY
SCOTT ADAMS
I'D LIKE YOU ALL TO MEET OUR NEW CO-OP EMPLOYEE.
WE DON'T PAY HIM. HE WORKS FOR FREE TO GAIN VALUABLE JOB EXPERIENCE.
I'M PUTTING YOU IN CHARGE OF THE PTG PROJECT!
WOW! WHAT IS IT?!!
PTG STANDS FOR "PAPER TOWEL GUY."
IF SOMEBODY SPILLS COFFEE IT'S YOUR JOB TO THROW YOUR BODY ON IT BEFORE IT REACHES ONE OF US.
OOPS
FIRE IN THE HOLE!!!
HOW'D I DO?
NOT SO GOOD, KID. THAT WAS TEA.
© 1995 United Feature Syndicate, Inc.

NOTES

JUNE/JULY

28 MONDAY

29 TUESDAY

30 WEDNESDAY

1 THURSDAY
CANADA DAY

FRIDAY 2

SATURDAY 3

SUNDAY 4
INDEPENDENCE DAY

JUNE

S	M	T	W	T	F	S
		1	2	3	4	5
6	7	8	9	10	11	12
13	14	15	16	17	18	19
20	21	22	23	24	25	26
27	28	29	30			

JULY

S	M	T	W	T	F	S
				1	2	3
4	5	6	7	8	9	10
11	12	13	14	15	16	17
18	19	20	21	22	23	24
25	26	27	28	29	30	31

DILBERT®
BY SCOTT ADAMS
WE DESPERATELY NEED ANOTHER PERSON ON MY PROJECT!
S. Adams
WE'RE ALREADY OVER HEADCOUNT. GET A CONTRACT EMPLOYEE.
OKAY, BUT THEY COST TWICE AS MUCH.
PLUS WE NEED TO BUY A COMPUTER.
RENT ONE. WE'RE OVER OUR CAPITAL BUDGET.
RENTING IS EXPENSIVE. WE'LL GO OVER OUR EXPENSE BUDGET.
I'LL FIRE WALLY. THAT WILL FREE UP SOME CASH.
WALLY'S ON MY PROJECT!
7/9
FORGET IT! I'LL JUST WORK SIXTEEN HOURS A DAY!!
THAT WORKED OUT PERFECTLY. I THINK I MIGHT BE A GENIUS OR SOMETHING.
© 1995 United Feature Syndicate, Inc.
I WONDER IF I SHOULD HAVE TOLD HIM THE PROJECT WAS CANCELLED LAST WEEK.

NOTES

JULY

5 MONDAY

6 TUESDAY

7 WEDNESDAY

8 THURSDAY

FRIDAY 9

SATURDAY 10

SUNDAY 11

JULY

S	M	T	W	T	F	S
				1	2	3
4	5	6	7	8	9	10
11	12	13	14	15	16	17
18	19	20	21	22	23	24
25	26	27	28	29	30	31

DILBERT®
BY
SCOTT ADAMS
I'VE DECIDED TO MAKE SOME CHANGES TO OUR CORPORATE CULTURE.
S. Adams
LET ME GUESS WHAT THAT MEANS.
WE'LL WORK LONGER HOURS WITHOUT EXTRA PAY...
YOUR MANAGEMENT STYLE WILL REMAIN EXACTLY THE SAME BECAUSE LORD KNOWS THERE'S NO NEED FOR YOU TO CHANGE.
WE'LL START CALLING OURSELVES A "TEAM" SO IT DOESN'T SEEM LIKE WORK!
I PREDICT THERE WILL BE VAPID SLOGANS PRINTED ON NOTEPADS, AND MAYBE SOME USELESS MEETINGS.
SHE'S PSYCHIC!
7-16
IS IT JUST ME OR IS THE CULTURE ALREADY CHANGING?
I FEEL IT! WE'RE CHANGING!
© 1995 United Feature Syndicate, Inc.
WHAT'S NEXT ON THE FAD MENU?
I WONDER IF IT'S TOO LATE TO RULE BY FEAR.

NOTES

JULY

12 MONDAY

13 TUESDAY

14 WEDNESDAY

15 THURSDAY

FRIDAY 16

SATURDAY 17

SUNDAY 18

JULY

S	M	T	W	T	F	S
				1	2	3
4	5	6	7	8	9	10
11	12	13	14	15	16	17
18	19	20	21	22	23	24
25	26	27	28	29	30	31

DILBERT®
BY
SCOTT ADAMS
I HAD A FEW SUGGESTIONS ON YOUR DOCUMENT, ALICE.
THANKS
BONK
S. Adams
I'VE MADE SOME UPGRADES TO YOUR DOCUMENT, ALICE.
THAT'S JUST WHAT IT NEEDED: A BUNCH OF OBTUSE ACRONYMS AND JARGON.
OOOH, LOOKY! YOU'VE ALSO MADE ELEGANT MULTI-TOPIC SENTENCES OUT OF MY STUBBY CLEAR ONES!
THANK YOU. AND PUT ME DOWN AS THE AUTHOR SINCE I'M THE BOSS.
MAYBE I SHOULD DISTRIBUTE LITTLE PLASTIC STATUES OF YOU WITH EVERY COPY. HOW ABOUT THAT?
7/23
© 1995 United Feature Syndicate, Inc.
HERE'S YOUR COPY, HERE'S YOUR STATUE, DON'T ASK.
OUR QUALITY IS LOW, BUT AT LEAST WE DON'T GET CREDIT.

NOTES

JULY

19 MONDAY

20 TUESDAY

21 WEDNESDAY

22 THURSDAY

FRIDAY 23

SATURDAY 24

SUNDAY 25

JULY

S	M	T	W	T	F	S
				1	2	3
4	5	6	7	8	9	10
11	12	13	14	15	16	17
18	19	20	21	22	23	24
25	26	27	28	29	30	31

DILBERT®
BY
SCOTT ADAMS
OUR NEW VP SAYS HE HAS AN "OPEN DOOR POLICY." LET'S CHECK IT OUT.
S. Adams
KNOCK KNOCK
HI HO. NOTHING IMPORTANT. WE JUST WANTED TO DROP IN.
THIS OPEN DOOR POLICY IS GREAT. OUR LAST VP WAS ALOOF.
ARE THOSE SOURBALLS?
LOOK AT ALL THE FURNITURE IN HERE!
I CALL COUCH!
IS THERE SOMETHING I CAN DO FOR YOU?
WELL... SOMETIMES OUR CUBICLES ARE TOO HOT.
COULD YOU HAVE SOMEBODY LOOK INTO IT?
7-30 © 1995 United Feature Syndicate, Inc.
BOY, THOSE SOURBALLS SURE LULL YOU INTO A FALSE SENSE OF SECURITY.
THE MAN IS LIKE A HUGE INSINCERE SPIDER.

NOTES

26 MONDAY

27 TUESDAY

28 WEDNESDAY

29 THURSDAY

FRIDAY 30

SATURDAY 31

SUNDAY 1

JULY

S	M	T	W	T	F	S
				1	2	3
4	5	6	7	8	9	10
11	12	13	14	15	16	17
18	19	20	21	22	23	24
25	26	27	28	29	30	31

AUGUST

S	M	T	W	T	F	S
1	2	3	4	5	6	7
8	9	10	11	12	13	14
15	16	17	18	19	20	21
22	23	24	25	26	27	28
29	30	31				

DILBERT®
BY
SCOTT ADAMS
WHEN DID YOU START BELIEVING THAT YOUR BOSS WAS AN EVIL ENTITY FROM ANOTHER DIMENSION?
S. Adams
I'D LIKE TO SIT IN ON YOUR CUSTOMER MEETING.
UH-OH
LET ME SHARE THE HIGH LEVEL STRATEGIC VIEW.
HERE WE GO.
LIFE BEGAN IN THE PRIMORDIAL STEW LITERALLY HUNDREDS OF YEARS AGO...
BUT WE ARE THE ONLY COMPANY WHO EVER FOUND SYNERGIES IN OUR WIN-WIN SOLUTIONS!
TWO HOURS LATER
AND WE WON'T STOP UNTIL WE DELIGHT EVERY CUSTOMER!
© 1995 United Feature Syndicate, Inc. (NYC)
8/6
I'D BE DELIGHTED IF YOU JUST TOLD ME ABOUT YOUR NEW INTERNET ACCESS PRODUCT.
I CANCELLED THE FUNDING YESTER-DAY.
WHO'S UP FOR A TOUR OF OUR CUBICLES?
GOTTA GO.

NOTES

AUGUST

2 MONDAY

3 TUESDAY

4 WEDNESDAY

5 THURSDAY

FRIDAY 6

SATURDAY 7

SUNDAY 8

AUGUST

S	M	T	W	T	F	S
1	2	3	4	5	6	7
8	9	10	11	12	13	14
15	16	17	18	19	20	21
22	23	24	25	26	27	28
29	30	31				

DILBERT®
BY SCOTT ADAMS
HERE'S HOW YOUR MARKETING DEPARTMENT CAN HELP RETAIN YOUR BEST ENGINEERS.
S. Adams
MARKETING GETS AN IDEA
WE'LL LEVERAGE OUR TECHNOLOGY BY BUILDING ANT FARMS.
SPREADSHEETS MAKE THE IDEA LOOK PROFITABLE.
THE ANT MILK ALONE WILL BE A POSITIVE NPV!
WHAT'S AN NPV?
WOW!
DON'T FORGET THE "WORST CASE SCENARIO."
WORST CASE, SOMEBODY BUILDS A GIGANTIC MAGNIFYING GLASS NEXT DOOR...
SOLUTION: BITE-SIZED ANT JERKY!
THERE'S NO RISK!
AN ENGINEER WILL BE ASSIGNED TO THE PROJECT.
ANT FARMS! DO IT!
UH-OH.
© 1995 United Feature Syndicate, Inc. (NYC)
8/13
THE ENGINEER WILL CHALLENGE THE ASSUMPTIONS
YOU CAN'T GET A GALLON OF MILK FROM AN ANT!
WHAT DO YOU KNOW ABOUT MARKETING?
RESULT: THE ENGINEER WILL NEVER LEAVE THE COMPANY.
SO... YOUR CURRENT JOB IS "ANT FARM ENGINEER"?
I'M DOOMED.

NOTES

AUGUST

9 MONDAY

10 TUESDAY

11 WEDNESDAY

12 THURSDAY

FRIDAY 13

SATURDAY 14

SUNDAY 15

AUGUST

S	M	T	W	T	F	S
1	2	3	4	5	6	7
8	9	10	11	12	13	14
15	16	17	18	19	20	21
22	23	24	25	26	27	28
29	30	31				

DILBERT®
BY
SCOTT ADAMS
PLEASE DON'T PROMISE THE PRODUCT MANAGER MORE THAN WE CAN DELIVER.
S. Adams
WE NEED A TOTALLY NEW SOFTWARE INTERFACE IN ONE MONTH.
YOU GOT IT!
AND REWRITE THE OPERATING SYSTEM SO WE DOMINATE THE INDUSTRY.
CONCURRENT DEVELOPMENT.
CHECK
SUDDENLY I FEEL OMNIPOTENT.
I WANT ALL NEW HARDWARE, ANTI-GRAVITY PACKAGING, HOLOGRAPHIC AGENTS...
YAWN YAWN
CAN YOUR TEAM REALLY DO THAT IN A MONTH?
LET ME GET THEIR REACTION.
© 1995 United Feature Syndicate, Inc. (NYC)
8/20
AAAGH!!
PESSIMISM WILL NOT LOOK GOOD ON YOUR PERFORMANCE REVIEW.
TWITCH

NOTES

AUGUST

16 MONDAY

17 TUESDAY

18 WEDNESDAY

19 THURSDAY

FRIDAY 20

SATURDAY 21

SUNDAY 22

AUGUST

S	M	T	W	T	F	S
1	2	3	4	5	6	7
8	9	10	11	12	13	14
15	16	17	18	19	20	21
22	23	24	25	26	27	28
29	30	31				

DILBERT®
BY
SCOTT ADAMS
I MADE A FEW CHANGES TO THE DESIGN.
S. Adams
WE'LL HAVE TO WORK AROUND THE CLOCK FOR MONTHS TO MAKE THESE CHANGES!!
WORK SMARTER, NOT HARDER.
8/27
YOU'RE TRYING TO VIOLATE THE LAWS OF PHYSICS!
RULES WERE MADE TO BE BROKEN.
THIS DESIGN WOULD CREATE ENOUGH RADIATION TO INSTANTLY KILL THE USER!!
BE SURE TO MENTION THAT IN THE DOCU-MENTATION.
LET'S WORK SMARTER NOT HARDER.
I THINK WE FOUND THE ONLY "BETA" TESTER WE'LL NEED.

NOTES

AUGUST

23 MONDAY

24 TUESDAY

25 WEDNESDAY

26 THURSDAY

FRIDAY 27

SATURDAY 28

SUNDAY 29

AUGUST

S	M	T	W	T	F	S
1	2	3	4	5	6	7
8	9	10	11	12	13	14
15	16	17	18	19	20	21
22	23	24	25	26	27	28
29	30	31				

DILBERT®
BY SCOTT ADAMS
MY LAPTOP PC KEEPS FREEZING UP. COME TAKE A LOOK AT IT.
S. Adams
I'M TELECOMMUTING, DOGBERT. I CAN'T BE DISTRACTED BY HOME PROJECTS.
DON'T COME ANOTHER STEP CLOSER. THIS IS MY VIRTUAL CUBICLE, WITHIN WHICH I CAN NOT BE DISTURBED.
THESE INVISIBLE WALLS FORM A CONE OF PRODUCTIVITY AROUND ME.
WITHIN THIS ZONE I AM A DEDICATED EMPLOYEE, TOTALLY FOCUSED ON THE CORPORATE VISION.
9/3
NOTHING CAN DISTRACT ME FROM MY FIRM COMMITMENT TO THE WORK-AT-HOME PRINCIPLE.
© 1995 United Feature Syndicate, Inc.(NYC)
FINE. I THINK I'LL SET THE COUCH ON FIRE.
ANOTHER VICTORY FOR THE DISTRACTOR!
I SWEAR, SOMEDAY PRINCIPLE WILL WIN!

NOTES

AUG/SEPT

30 MONDAY

31 TUESDAY

1 WEDNESDAY

2 THURSDAY

FRIDAY 3

SATURDAY 4

SUNDAY 5

AUGUST

S	M	T	W	T	F	S
1	2	3	4	5	6	7
8	9	10	11	12	13	14
15	16	17	18	19	20	21
22	23	24	25	26	27	28
29	30	31				

SEPTEMBER

S	M	T	W	T	F	S
			1	2	3	4
5	6	7	8	9	10	11
12	13	14	15	16	17	18
19	20	21	22	23	24	25
26	27	28	29	30		

DILBERT®
BY
SCOTT ADAMS
WE JUST HIRED JACK AWAY FROM OUR COMPETITOR. HE WAS THEIR BEST MANAGER.
S. ADAMS
JACK WILL BE IN CHARGE OF PROJECT "GOOSEFOOD."
I'D LIKE YOU TWO TO BRIEF JACK ON THE PROJECT.
PROJECT "GOOSEFOOD" HAS NO BUDGET AND NO MANAGEMENT SUPPORT.
YOUR JOB IS TO BUILD A GLOBAL INFORMATION NETWORK IN TWO WEEKS.
FAILURE IS CERTAIN. SOON YOU WILL LEAVE THE INDUSTRY IN DISGRACE.
9/10
© 1995 United Feature Syndicate, Inc. (NYC)
. . . JUST LIKE THE OTHER "BEST MANAGERS" WE HIRED FROM OUR COMPETITORS.
JUST OUT OF CURIOSITY, HOW DID THE PROJECT GET ITS NAME?
LET'S JUST SAY THAT YOU'RE THE GOOSE FOOD . . .

NOTES

SEPTEMBER

6 MONDAY
LABOR DAY

7 TUESDAY

8 WEDNESDAY

9 THURSDAY

FRIDAY 10

SATURDAY 11
ROSH HASHANAH

SUNDAY 12

SEPTEMBER

S	M	T	W	T	F	S
			1	2	3	4
5	6	7	8	9	10	11
12	13	14	15	16	17	18
19	20	21	22	23	24	25
26	27	28	29	30		

DILBERT®
BY
SCOTT ADAMS
IT'S TIME FOR MARKETING TO PUT THE GLITTER ON THIS SOFTWARE YOU'VE CREATED.
S.Adams
WITH MY GUIDANCE THIS WILL BECOME THE PREMIER DATA BACKUP SOFTWARE!
BEAR IN MIND THAT WE SAID IT WOULD TAKE SIX MONTHS TO WRITE IT.
YOU ONLY GAVE US A MONTH.
WE'LL FIX THE BUGS IN THE NEXT RELEASE.
TELL ME ABOUT THE FEATURES.
AT THIS POINT ALL IT DOES IS ERASE YOUR DISK DRIVE.
UNLESS YOU'RE ON A NETWORK.
WHAT HAPPENS IF YOU'RE ON A NETWORK?
IT ERASES EVERYBODY'S DISK DRIVES.
9/17
© 1995 United Feature Syndicate, Inc.(NYC)
AND HEAVEN HELP YOU IF YOU HAVE A MODEM...
IT CALLS ALL YOUR FRIENDS AND ERASES THEIR PCs.
WE'LL CALL IT "QuikProtect."
IF YOU HAVE A SOUND CARD IT SWEARS AT YOU.

NOTES

SEPTEMBER

13 MONDAY

14 TUESDAY

15 WEDNESDAY

16 THURSDAY

FRIDAY 17

SATURDAY 18

SUNDAY 19

SEPTEMBER

S	M	T	W	T	F	S
			1	2	3	4
5	6	7	8	9	10	11
12	13	14	15	16	17	18
19	20	21	22	23	24	25
26	27	28	29	30		

DILBERT®
BY
SCOTT ADAMS
I HAVE TO TAKE A CONTRACT TO OUR COMPANY LAWYER. I NEED YOUR HELP, DOGBERT.
S. Adams
PLEASE REVIEW THIS CONTRACT. I NEED IT TODAY.
GIVE ME ALL OF YOUR COPIES PLUS THE ORIGINAL. THEN GO AWAY.
9/24
DON'T DO IT! HE PLANS TO LOSE THEM!!
GOOD DOG!
DANG!
I CANNOT APPROVE THIS. SOMEBODY MIGHT SUE US FOR NO GOOD REASON.
THAT'S TRUE WITH ANY CONTRACT. ISN'T HE USING ABSURD LOGIC?
LET'S FIND OUT.
© 1995 United Feature Syndicate, Inc.(NYC)
APPROVE THE CONTRACT NOW OR I'LL SUE YOU FOR OBSTRUCTION OF DOGS!!
OKAY OKAY
WOW
THE GREAT THING ABOUT ABSURD LOGIC IS THAT IT FITS ANY SITUATION.

NOTES

SEPTEMBER

20 MONDAY
YOM KIPPUR

21 TUESDAY

22 WEDNESDAY

23 THURSDAY

FRIDAY 24

SATURDAY 25

SUNDAY 26

SEPTEMBER

S	M	T	W	T	F	S
			1	2	3	4
5	6	7	8	9	10	11
12	13	14	15	16	17	18
19	20	21	22	23	24	25
26	27	28	29	30		

DILBERT®
BY
SCOTT ADAMS
WISH ME LUCK, DOGBERT.
IF YOU GET MORE LUCK, WOULDN'T THERE BE LESS LUCK AVAILABLE FOR ME?
S. Adams
FOR "DESIRED SALARY" YOU WROTE "ONE MILLION DOLLARS."
YES, THANKS FOR ASKING.
10-1
PERHAPS THE QUESTION IS MISLEADING. THE APPLICATION SHOULD HAVE ASKED WHAT SALARY YOU EXPECT.
OH... WELL, I EXPECT YOU'LL HIRE SOMEBODY MORE QUALIFIED AND MY SALARY WILL REMAIN UNCHANGED.
NO, TOO HONEST. I'M LOOKING FOR SOMETHING CLOSE TO REALITY, WITH MAYBE TWENTY-PERCENT FANTASY LAYERED ON TOP.
OKAY... I'D LIKE A FIFTEEN-PERCENT RAISE AND A LITTLE SHOULDER MASSAGE.
WHY DOES IT SEEM THAT I'M THE ONLY HONEST GUY ON EARTH?
YOUR TYPE TENDS NOT TO REPRODUCE.

NOTES

SEPT/OCT

27 MONDAY

28 TUESDAY

29 WEDNESDAY

30 THURSDAY

FRIDAY 1

SATURDAY 2

SUNDAY 3

SEPTEMBER

S	M	T	W	T	F	S
			1	2	3	4
5	6	7	8	9	10	11
12	13	14	15	16	17	18
19	20	21	22	23	24	25
26	27	28	29	30		

OCTOBER

S	M	T	W	T	F	S
					1	2
3	4	5	6	7	8	9
10	11	12	13	14	15	16
17	18	19	20	21	22	23
24	25	26	27	28	29	30
31						

DILBERT®
BY
SCOTT ADAMS
THAT'S FOUR HOURS THAT I'D LIKE TO HAVE BACK.
WHO CALLED THAT MEETING ANYWAY?
S. Adams
I MUST HAVE LEFT MY CALENDAR IN THERE.
OOOH
?
I'VE DISCOVERED A PRIMITIVE DONUT-SCAVENGING MAN CLAD ONLY IN YELLOW STICKY NOTES!!
10-8
I WAS ONCE LIKE YOU, BEFORE THE GREAT RIF.
BUT RATHER THAN LEAVE IN HUMILIATION I DECIDED TO STAY AND LIVE OFF THE LAND LIKE OUR PROUD ANCESTORS.
© 1995 United Feature Syndicate, Inc.(NYC)
TO ENSURE A BOUNTIFUL HARVEST I DO MY DONUT DANCE TO THE GODS.
WHEN THAT DOESN'T WORK I DISTRIBUTE MEETING NOTICES.
YOU'RE THE ONE!!

NOTES

OCTOBER

4 MONDAY

5 TUESDAY

6 WEDNESDAY

7 THURSDAY

FRIDAY 8

SATURDAY 9

SUNDAY 10

OCTOBER

S	M	T	W	T	F	S
					1	2
3	4	5	6	7	8	9
10	11	12	13	14	15	16
17	18	19	20	21	22	23
24	25	26	27	28	29	30
31						

DILBERT
BY
SCOTT ADAMS
WHY DO YOU WANT TO BE OUR NEW "LONG RANGE PLANNER," MISTER DOGBERT?
S. Adams
BECAUSE "LONG RANGE" IS VERY FAR AWAY . . .
. . . THEREFORE IT WILL BE IMPOSSIBLE TO EVALUATE MY PERFORMANCE.
10-15
IF IT'S NOT TOO MUCH TO ASK, I'D LIKE TO BE ON FLEX-TIME SO YOU'LL NEVER KNOW IF I'M SUPPOSED TO BE AT WORK.
I'LL NEED AN INTERNET CONNECTION AT HOME SO I CAN TELECOMMUTE AND NOT POLLUTE.
BECAUSE I GIVE A HOOT.
ALSO, I'D LIKE TO BE IN A GROUP WITH LOTS OF LOSERS. THAT WAY I'LL GET THE BIGGEST RAISE WHEN WE'RE RANKED.
© 1995 United Feature Syndicate, Inc.(NYC)
YOU'RE HIRED. ALL OF THE OTHER APPLICANTS DEMANDED RELOCATION EXPENSES AND I HAVE NO BUDGET FOR THAT.
WHY DO I HAVE TO WORK WHILE YOU JUST LOOK FOR POODLE GRAPHICS ON THE INTERNET?
DON'T WORK TOO HARD; I'D LIKE A BIG RAISE.

NOTES

OCTOBER

11 MONDAY

COLUMBUS DAY
THANKSGIVING (CANADA)

12 TUESDAY

13 WEDNESDAY

14 THURSDAY

FRIDAY 15

SATURDAY 16

NATIONAL BOSS DAY

SUNDAY 17

OCTOBER

S	M	T	W	T	F	S
					1	2
3	4	5	6	7	8	9
10	11	12	13	14	15	16
17	18	19	20	21	22	23
24	25	26	27	28	29	30
31						

DILBERT
BY
SCOTT ADAMS
THIS GRAPHIC SHOWS OUR BIGGEST OBSTACLE TO SUCCESS.
S. Adams
RDS ZPL ABP
NDP QRT LNP
?
?
?
ARE YOU SAYING OUR BIGGEST OBSTACLE TO SUCCESS IS POOR GRAPHICS?
I THINK HE'S SAYING OUR BIGGEST PROBLEM IS HIS OVERALL INABILITY TO COMMUNICATE.
I THINK HIS POINT GOES BEYOND COMMUNICATION. HE'S SHOWING US THAT HE DOESN'T EVEN THINK CLEARLY!
THAT'S IT!
© 1995 United Feature Syndicate, Inc.(NYC)
10/22
HIGH FIVE!!
YOU BROKE THE CODE!
YOU KNOW HOW I SAID YOU SHOULD PARTICIPATE MORE IN MEETINGS?
I DIDN'T MEAN IT.

NOTES

OCTOBER

18 MONDAY

19 TUESDAY

20 WEDNESDAY

21 THURSDAY

FRIDAY 22

SATURDAY 23

SUNDAY 24

OCTOBER

S	M	T	W	T	F	S
					1	2
3	4	5	6	7	8	9
10	11	12	13	14	15	16
17	18	19	20	21	22	23
24	25	26	27	28	29	30
31						

DILBERT®
BY
SCOTT ADAMS
HELEN, DO YOU HAVE ANY STAPLES IN THE SUPPLY CABINET?
S. Adams
NO, I ONLY STOCK THE BASICS: CHEAP PENS WITH GREEN INK, BIG JARS OF GLUE AND RIBBONS FOR OBSOLETE PRINTERS.
COULD YOU ORDER SOME STAPLES?
YOU NEED TO GIVE ME THE ORDER NUMBER.
OKAY. CAN I SEE YOUR SUPPLY CATALOG?
WALLY BORROWED IT.
I'D BETTER GET THAT; IT MIGHT BE PERSONAL.
RRRING
SOB
WALLY, DO YOU HAVE THE...
I NEED YOUR HELP WITH THIS. PULL UP A CHAIR.
© 1996 United Feature Syndicate, Inc.(NYC)
10/29
I NEED BOTH OF YOU TO COME TALK TO A VENDOR THAT WE'LL NEVER USE.
THANKS TO TEAMWORK, I ALMOST STAPLED SOMETHING TODAY.
I'M SO PROUD TO KNOW YOU.

NOTES

OCTOBER

25 MONDAY

26 TUESDAY

27 WEDNESDAY

28 THURSDAY

FRIDAY 29

SATURDAY 30

SUNDAY 31

HALLOWEEN

OCTOBER

S	M	T	W	T	F	S
					1	2
3	4	5	6	7	8	9
10	11	12	13	14	15	16
17	18	19	20	21	22	23
24	25	26	27	28	29	30
31						

DILBERT®
BY
SCOTT ADAMS
I WORKED ALL NIGHT BUT I FINISHED THE PRESENTATION PACKAGE YOU WANTED.
S. Adams
PUT THE PRESENTATION DATE ON EACH PAGE.
THOSE ARE COLOR TRANSPARENCIES. IT WOULD TAKE HOURS AND COST HUNDREDS OF DOLLARS TO REPRINT THEM.
11/5
THERE'S NO REASON TO DATE THEM. IN FACT, IT WOULD LIMIT FUTURE USE AND CLUTTER THE PAGE.
BUT SINCE YOU'RE INCAPABLE OF ADMITTING ERROR...
I EAGERLY AWAIT YOUR BIZARRE, OTHER-WORLDLY EXPLANATION FOR PUTTING THE DATE ON EACH PAGE.
© 1995 United Feature Syndicate, Inc.(NYC)
SOME PEOPLE MIGHT NOT HAVE CALENDARS. AND WE HAVE TO MAKE SURE IT'S NOT A HOLIDAY.
BAM!
OUCH. MY BRAIN EXPLODED.
THE FIRST PRESENTATION IS FEBRUARY 30TH...

NOTES

NOVEMBER

1 MONDAY

2 TUESDAY
ELECTION DAY

3 WEDNESDAY

4 THURSDAY

FRIDAY 5

SATURDAY 6

SUNDAY 7

NOVEMBER

S	M	T	W	T	F	S
	1	2	3	4	5	6
7	8	9	10	11	12	13
14	15	16	17	18	19	20
21	22	23	24	25	26	27
28	29	30				

DILBERT®
BY
SCOTT ADAMS
MISTER CATBERT WILL EXPLAIN OUR NEW "TOTAL COMPENSATION PLAN" FOR EXCELLENCE.
S. Adams
WE NO LONGER VIEW COMPENSATION IN THE NARROW TERMS OF SALARY ALONE.
DANGER! DANGER!
IF EMPLOYEE BENEFITS GO UP, THEN SALARIES CAN GO DOWN AND IT ALL BALANCES OUT.
11/12
FOR EXAMPLE, DID YOU KNOW YOU COULD LOWER YOUR BLOOD PRESSURE BY RUBBING MY SOFT, FURRY BELLY?
IT MIGHT BE A TRICK!
WHAT'S THE WORST THING THAT COULD HAPPEN?
© 1995 United Feature Syndicate, Inc.(NYC)
HA HA HA!!! IT'S A HEALTH BENEFIT! NOW I'LL CUT EVERYBODY'S SALARY!
I'VE NOTICED THAT THE MORE HEALTH BENEFITS I GET, THE WORSE I FEEL.

NOTES

NOVEMBER

8 MONDAY

9 TUESDAY

10 WEDNESDAY

11 THURSDAY
VETERANS' DAY
REMEMBRANCE DAY (CANADA)

FRIDAY 12

SATURDAY 13

SUNDAY 14

NOVEMBER

S	M	T	W	T	F	S
	1	2	3	4	5	6
7	8	9	10	11	12	13
14	15	16	17	18	19	20
21	22	23	24	25	26	27
28	29	30				

DILBERT®
BY
SCOTT ADAMS
WE NEED TO SHIP THE V-1 PRODUCT TOMORROW. I PROMISED OUR CEO HE CAN ANNOUNCE IT AT THE SHAREHOLDER MEETING.
S. Adams
THAT'S TWO MONTHS EARLY!!
WE HAVEN'T ADDED ANY FEATURES YET!!
WHAT WOULD WE SHIP? OUR LAB PROTOTYPE IS THE ONLY V-1 IN EXISTENCE!
NO...YOU WOULDN'T!
I'VE SCHEDULED PRESS TOURS SO YOU CAN DO DEMOS ALL NEXT WEEK.
ON WHAT?!
WE'LL NEED TWENTY THOUSAND DOLLARS TO BUILD ANOTHER PROTOTYPE!
THAT REMINDS ME; I FROZE THE BUDGET FOR THE REST OF THE YEAR.
11/19
© 1995 United Feature Syndicate, Inc. (NYC)
IF THERE'S ANYTHING YOU'D LIKE ME TO DO, DON'T HESITATE TO ASK.
YEAH, I'D LIKE YOU TO DO SOME-THING...
OOH... I THINK I SHOULD HAVE HESITATED TO ASK THAT.

NOTES

NOVEMBER

15 MONDAY

16 TUESDAY

17 WEDNESDAY

18 THURSDAY

FRIDAY 19

SATURDAY 20

SUNDAY 21

NOVEMBER

S	M	T	W	T	F	S
	1	2	3	4	5	6
7	8	9	10	11	12	13
14	15	16	17	18	19	20
21	22	23	24	25	26	27
28	29	30				

DILBERT®
BY
SCOTT ADAMS
THE CLEVER SALES-MAN EVALUATES HIS PREY.
BADGE
VISITORS SIGN IN
S. Adams
I HOPE HE'S AN IMPORTANT DECISION-MAKER.
TAKE ANY SEAT. I CALL THE GOOD CHAIR.
WARNING! CUBICLE! LOW-RANKING EMPLOYEE!
HERE'S OUR ORGANIZATION CHART: PRESIDENT... SENIOR VICE PRESIDENT... VICE PRESIDENT...
OKAY, LIFT YOUR FOOT. DO YOU SEE THAT COFFEE STAIN ON THE CARPET?
THAT'S YOU?
NO, THAT'S MY BOSS. I WOULD BE UNDER THE CARPET.
11/26
© 1995 United Feature Syndicate, Inc.(NYC)
DO I HAVE ANY HOPE OF TALKING TO SOMEBODY WHO CAN MAKE A DECISION?
LET ME CHECK.
HEY, WALLY. WHAT'S A "DECISION"?
IT SOUNDS LIKE SOMETHING OUR COMPETITORS DO.
SOB

NOTES

NOVEMBER

22 MONDAY

23 TUESDAY

24 WEDNESDAY

25 THURSDAY

THANKSGIVING

FRIDAY 26

SATURDAY 27

SUNDAY 28

NOVEMBER

S	M	T	W	T	F	S
	1	2	3	4	5	6
7	8	9	10	11	12	13
14	15	16	17	18	19	20
21	22	23	24	25	26	27
28	29	30				

DILBERT®
BY
SCOTT ADAMS
WORKING LATE AGAIN, HUH, ALICE?
SEVENTY HOURS THIS WEEK...
S. Adams
ME TOO. THANK GOODNESS FOR OVERTIME PAY!
OVERTIME PAY?
ALLOW ME TO EXPLAIN.
UNLIKE YOU SO-CALLED "EXEMPT" EMPLOYEES, MY INCOME INCREASES IF I WORK ADDITIONAL HOURS.
$
Hours
I'M PULLING IN SEVENTY-FIVE THOUSAND A YEAR. AND HALF THE TIME I JUST HIDE IN THE BASEMENT READING "FISHING" MAGAZINE.
© 1995 United Feature Syndicate, Inc.(NYC)
THE ONLY DOWN SIDE IS THAT I DON'T GET TO ENJOY THE INTELLECTUAL STIMULATION OF MY CO-WORKERS THE WAY YOU DO.
12/3
I DON'T KNOW WHAT I LIKE BETTER — DEEP SEA FISHING OR CUBICLE FISHING.
FISH

NOTES

NOV/DEC

29 MONDAY

30 TUESDAY

1 WEDNESDAY

2 THURSDAY

FRIDAY 3

SATURDAY 4
HANUKKAH

SUNDAY 5

NOVEMBER

S	M	T	W	T	F	S
	1	2	3	4	5	6
7	8	9	10	11	12	13
14	15	16	17	18	19	20
21	22	23	24	25	26	27
28	29	30				

DECEMBER

S	M	T	W	T	F	S
			1	2	3	4
5	6	7	8	9	10	11
12	13	14	15	16	17	18
19	20	21	22	23	24	25
26	27	28	29	30	31	

DILBERT®
BY
SCOTT ADAMS
HELLO, IS THIS THE "HELP DESK"?
NO, THAT GROUP GOT REENGINEERED OUT OF EXISTENCE.
S. Adams
I'M THE NEW "NO HELP WHATSOEVER DESK." MY JOB IS TO MAKE SURE YOU NEVER CALL AGAIN.
12/10
CAN YOU TELL ME HOW TO MAKE A PIE CHART?
CRUSH YOUR COMPUTER INTO SMALL CHUNKS, ADD FLOUR AND BAKE ONE HOUR.
WHILE YOU'RE WAITING, READ THE FREE NOVEL WE SENT YOU. IT'S A SPANISH STORY ABOUT A GUY NAMED "MANUAL."
© 1995 United Feature Syndicate, Inc.(NYC)
REPEAT THE PROCESS UNTIL YOU GET THE DESIRED RESULT.
THIS LOST A LOT IN THE TRANSLATION.
MANUAL

NOTES

DECEMBER

6 MONDAY

7 TUESDAY

8 WEDNESDAY

9 THURSDAY

FRIDAY 10

SATURDAY 11

SUNDAY 12

DECEMBER

S	M	T	W	T	F	S
			1	2	3	4
5	6	7	8	9	10	11
12	13	14	15	16	17	18
19	20	21	22	23	24	25
26	27	28	29	30	31	

DILBERT®
BY
SCOTT ADAMS
ALICE, OUR RECORDS SHOW THAT YOU HAVEN'T TAKEN A VACATION ALL YEAR.
S. Adams
COMPANY POLICY REQUIRES YOU TO USE YOUR VACATION DAYS.
HOW?? YOU TOLD ME TO WORK SEVEN DAYS A WEEK TO PREPARE THE PROJECT FOR YOUR BOSS'S YEAR-END REVIEW.
12/17
DO YOU WANT ME TO MEET THE ARTIFICIAL PROJECT TARGET OR THE ARTIFICIAL VACATION TARGET?
HELLO!!! THESE ARE MUTUALLY EXCLUSIVE GOALS!!! HELLO!!!
OOH... SORRY. I USUALLY JUST THINK THAT LAST PART IN SILENT FRUSTRATION.
© 1995 United Feature Syndicate, Inc.(NYC)
MOVING RIGHT ALONG... KUDOS TO WALLY FOR USING ALL OF HIS VACATION DAYS AHEAD OF SCHEDULE.
GET OVER IT, ALICE. WE CAN'T ALL BE SUPERSTARS.

NOTES

DECEMBER

13 MONDAY

14 TUESDAY

15 WEDNESDAY

16 THURSDAY

FRIDAY 17

SATURDAY 18

SUNDAY 19

DECEMBER

S	M	T	W	T	F	S
			1	2	3	4
5	6	7	8	9	10	11
12	13	14	15	16	17	18
19	20	21	22	23	24	25
26	27	28	29	30	31	

DILBERT®
BY
SCOTT ADAMS
Happy Airlines
S. Adams
VACATION, HERE WE COME!
CLICK CLICK CLICK CLICK CLICK CLICK CLICK CLICK CLICK CLICK
WHY DO THEY HAVE TO ENTER SO MUCH STUFF IN THE COMPUTER?
CLICK CLICK CLICK CLICK CLICK CLICK CLICK
THEY ALREADY HAVE OUR RESERVATION AND SEAT ASSIGNMENT IN THERE. WHAT ELSE DO THEY NEED?
CLICK CLICK CLICK CLICK CLICK CLICK
12/24
I'M DEVELOPING A SUDDEN FEAR OF FLYING.
CLICK CLICK CLICK CLICK CLICK CLICK CLICK CLICK CLICK CLICK CLICK
STEP ASIDE.
WHAT'S GOING ON UP HERE??!!
GATE 13. HAVE A NICE FLIGHT.
OKAY.
"THEY NEVER SAW THEIR BELOVED LUGGAGE AGAIN. THE MISFITS ALWAYS REGRETTED OFFENDING TANTRA, THE GODDESS OF FLIGHT. THE END."
CLICK CLICK CLICK CLICK

NOTES

DECEMBER

20 MONDAY

21 TUESDAY

22 WEDNESDAY

23 THURSDAY

FRIDAY 24

SATURDAY 25
CHRISTMAS

SUNDAY 26
BOXING DAY (CANADA)

DECEMBER

S	M	T	W	T	F	S
			1	2	3	4
5	6	7	8	9	10	11
12	13	14	15	16	17	18
19	20	21	22	23	24	25
26	27	28	29	30	31	

DILBERT®
BY
SCOTT ADAMS
I'VE GOT AN IDEA!
WE'RE DOOMED.
S. Adams
WHY CAN'T WE RUN OUR INVENTORY DATABASE OVER OUR E-MAIL SYSTEM?
FACT: THAT IS THE STUPIDEST IDEA IN THE UNIVERSE.
12/31
FACT: HIS COMPRE-HENSION IS SO LIMITED THAT DEBATE IS FUTILE.
FACT: WE COULD SPEND HOURS UNSUCCESSFULLY EXPLAINING WHY IT'S A STUPID IDEA.
FACT: HE WOULD NEVER KNOW IF WE USED HIS IDEA OR NOT.
© 1995 United Feature Syndicate, Inc. (NYC)
NO PROBLEM.
WE'LL GET RIGHT ON IT.
MY WORK IS DONE.
STUPIDITY IS LIKE NUCLEAR POWER; IT CAN BE USED FOR GOOD OR EVIL.
AND YOU DON'T WANT TO GET ANY ON YOU.

NOTES

DEC/JAN

27 MONDAY

28 TUESDAY

29 WEDNESDAY

30 THURSDAY

FRIDAY 31

SATURDAY 1
NEW YEAR'S DAY

SUNDAY 2

DECEMBER

S	M	T	W	T	F	S
			1	2	3	4
5	6	7	8	9	10	11
12	13	14	15	16	17	18
19	20	21	22	23	24	25
26	27	28	29	30	31	

JANUARY 2000

S	M	T	W	T	F	S
						1
2	3	4	5	6	7	8
9	10	11	12	13	14	15
16	17	18	19	20	21	22
23	24	25	26	27	28	29
30	31					

2000

JANUARY

FEBRUARY

MARCH

APRIL

MAY

JUNE

JULY

AUGUST

SEPTEMBER

OCTOBER

NOVEMBER

DECEMBER

1998

JANUARY

S	M	T	W	T	F	S
				1	2	3
4	5	6	7	8	9	10
11	12	13	14	15	16	17
18	19	20	21	22	23	24
25	26	27	28	29	30	31

FEBRUARY

S	M	T	W	T	F	S
1	2	3	4	5	6	7
8	9	10	11	12	13	14
15	16	17	18	19	20	21
22	23	24	25	26	27	28

MARCH

S	M	T	W	T	F	S
1	2	3	4	5	6	7
8	9	10	11	12	13	14
15	16	17	18	19	20	21
22	23	24	25	26	27	28
29	30	31				

APRIL

S	M	T	W	T	F	S
			1	2	3	4
5	6	7	8	9	10	11
12	13	14	15	16	17	18
19	20	21	22	23	24	25
26	27	28	29	30		

MAY

S	M	T	W	T	F	S
					1	2
3	4	5	6	7	8	9
10	11	12	13	14	15	16
17	18	19	20	21	22	23
24	25	26	27	28	29	30
31						

JUNE

S	M	T	W	T	F	S
	1	2	3	4	5	6
7	8	9	10	11	12	13
14	15	16	17	18	19	20
21	22	23	24	25	26	27
28	29	30				

JULY

S	M	T	W	T	F	S
			1	2	3	4
5	6	7	8	9	10	11
12	13	14	15	16	17	18
19	20	21	22	23	24	25
26	27	28	29	30	31	

AUGUST

S	M	T	W	T	F	S
						1
2	3	4	5	6	7	8
9	10	11	12	13	14	15
16	17	18	19	20	21	22
23	24	25	26	27	28	29
30	31					

SEPTEMBER

S	M	T	W	T	F	S
		1	2	3	4	5
6	7	8	9	10	11	12
13	14	15	16	17	18	19
20	21	22	23	24	25	26
27	28	29	30			

OCTOBER

S	M	T	W	T	F	S
				1	2	3
4	5	6	7	8	9	10
11	12	13	14	15	16	17
18	19	20	21	22	23	24
25	26	27	28	29	30	31

NOVEMBER

S	M	T	W	T	F	S
1	2	3	4	5	6	7
8	9	10	11	12	13	14
15	16	17	18	19	20	21
22	23	24	25	26	27	28
29	30					

DECEMBER

S	M	T	W	T	F	S
		1	2	3	4	5
6	7	8	9	10	11	12
13	14	15	16	17	18	19
20	21	22	23	24	25	26
27	28	29	30	31		

2000

JANUARY

S	M	T	W	T	F	S
						1
2	3	4	5	6	7	8
9	10	11	12	13	14	15
16	17	18	19	20	21	22
23	24	25	26	27	28	29
30	31					

FEBRUARY

S	M	T	W	T	F	S
		1	2	3	4	5
6	7	8	9	10	11	12
13	14	15	16	17	18	19
20	21	22	23	24	25	26
27	28	29				

MARCH

S	M	T	W	T	F	S
			1	2	3	4
5	6	7	8	9	10	11
12	13	14	15	16	17	18
19	20	21	22	23	24	25
26	27	28	29	30	31	

APRIL

S	M	T	W	T	F	S
						1
2	3	4	5	6	7	8
9	10	11	12	13	14	15
16	17	18	19	20	21	22
23	24	25	26	27	28	29
30						

MAY

S	M	T	W	T	F	S
	1	2	3	4	5	6
7	8	9	10	11	12	13
14	15	16	17	18	19	20
21	22	23	24	25	26	27
28	29	30	31			

JUNE

S	M	T	W	T	F	S
				1	2	3
4	5	6	7	8	9	10
11	12	13	14	15	16	17
18	19	20	21	22	23	24
25	26	27	28	29	30	

JULY

S	M	T	W	T	F	S
						1
2	3	4	5	6	7	8
9	10	11	12	13	14	15
16	17	18	19	20	21	22
23	24	25	26	27	28	29
30	31					

AUGUST

S	M	T	W	T	F	S
		1	2	3	4	5
6	7	8	9	10	11	12
13	14	15	16	17	18	19
20	21	22	23	24	25	26
27	28	29	30	31		

SEPTEMBER

S	M	T	W	T	F	S
					1	2
3	4	5	6	7	8	9
10	11	12	13	14	15	16
17	18	19	20	21	22	23
24	25	26	27	28	29	30

OCTOBER

S	M	T	W	T	F	S
1	2	3	4	5	6	7
8	9	10	11	12	13	14
15	16	17	18	19	20	21
22	23	24	25	26	27	28
29	30	31				

NOVEMBER

S	M	T	W	T	F	S
			1	2	3	4
5	6	7	8	9	10	11
12	13	14	15	16	17	18
19	20	21	22	23	24	25
26	27	28	29	30		

DECEMBER

S	M	T	W	T	F	S
					1	2
3	4	5	6	7	8	9
10	11	12	13	14	15	16
17	18	19	20	21	22	23
24	25	26	27	28	29	30
31						